# Mad 4 Maths
## 3rd Class

**Len and Anne Frobisher**

© Len and Anne Frobisher 2002
Under Licence from Pearson Education Limited
Original title published as Maths Plus Word Problems

This book is copyright and reproduction of the whole or part without the Publisher's written permission is prohibited.

This edition published by Carroll Education Limited

http://www.carrolleducation.ie

Designers: DP Press Ltd, Sevenoaks, Kent and M & J Graphics, Harold's Cross, Dublin

Illustrators: Garry Davies and Nicola Sedgwick

Cover Illustrator: Andrew Hunt

ISBN: 978-184450-142-7

All rights reserved. No part of this publication may be reproduced, stored in a retrieval system, or transmitted in any form or by any means, electronic, mechanical, photocopying, recording or otherwise, without either the prior permission of the Publisher or a licence permitting restricted copying in Ireland issued by the Irish Copyright Licensing Agency, 25 Denzille Lane, Dublin 2

# Contents

| UNIT | TOPIC | PAGE |
|---|---|---|

## Autumn 1st half term

1. Number problems 1 . . . . . . . 4
2. Money problems 1 . . . . . . . . 5
3. Number problems 2 . . . . . . . 6
4. Time problems 1 . . . . . . . . . 7
5. Number problems 3 . . . . . . . 8
6. Length problems 1 . . . . . . . . 9
7. Review problems 1 . . . . . . . 10

## Autumn 2nd half term

8. Number problems 4 . . . . . . .12
9. Money problems 2 . . . . . . . .13
10. Number problems 5 . . . . . .14
11. Number problems 6 . . . . . .15
12. Time problems 2 . . . . . . . . .16
13. Number problems 7 . . . . . .17
14. Review problems 2 . . . . . .18

## Spring 1st half term

1. Number problems 8 . . . . . .20
2. Money problems 3 . . . . . . .21
3. Number problems 9 . . . . . .22
4. Time problems 3 . . . . . . . .23
5. Weight problems 1 . . . . . . .24
6. Measures problems 1 . . . .25
7. Review problems 3 . . . . . .26

## Spring 2nd half term

8. Number problems 10 . . . . .28
9. Money problems 4 . . . . . . .29
10. Number problems 11 . . . . .30
11. Number problems 12 . . . . .31
12. Number problems 13 . . . . .32
13. Review problems 4 . . . . . .33

## Summer 1st half term

1. Number problems 14 . . . . .34
2. Money problems 5 . . . . . . .35
3. Number problems 15 . . . . .36
4. Capacity problems 1 . . . . .37
5. Measures problems 2 . . . .38
6. Measures problems 3 . . . .39
7. Review problems 5 . . . . . .40

## Summer 2nd half term

8. Number problems 16 . . . . 42
9. Money problems 6 . . . . . . 43
10. Number problems 17 . . . . 44
11. Number problems 18 . . . . 45
12. Time problems 4 . . . . . . . . 46
13. Number problems 19 . . . . 47
14. Review problems 6 . . . . . . 48

# Number problems 1

**1** Jane has 2 books of 100 stickers, 1 book of 10 stickers and 5 single stickers.

How many stickers has she altogether?

**2** There are 9 crayons in a red box and 16 in a blue box.

Which box has more crayons?
How many more?

**3** Eoin estimates that there are 60 marbles in a jar.

Anna thinks there are 10 more that that. What is Anna's estimate?

**4** Between pages 248 and 251 some pages are missing.

What are the numbers of the missing pages?

**5** Four runners in a race have the numbers 198, 918, 819 and 891.

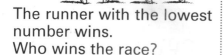

The runner with the lowest number wins.
Who wins the race?

**6** Robert has 481 stamps in a large book. He puts 100 of them into a smaller book.

How many stamps are left in the larger book?

**7**  *I am an odd number. I am between 48 and 51.* What am I?

# Money problems 1

**1** On a cake stall buns cost 4c each.

Aoife buys 5 buns.
How much do the five buns cost her?
She pays with a 50c coin.
How much change does she get?

**2** The comic Blitz costs €2.

Jakub buys two Blitz comics.
What change does he get from a €5 note?

**3** Animal badges cost 3c each.
Steve wants to buy four badges.
How much money does he need?

**4** For her birthday Alice is given two €5 notes.
How much money is she given altogether?

**5** In her purse Katie has three 2c coins.

How much has she in her purse?

**6** Each week James saves a 5c coin. Altogether he has saved 25c.

For how many weeks has he saved?

**7**

I am a round, gold coin.
I am between 5c and 20c.

What am I?
10c

# Number problems 2

**1** In a packet there are 24 daffodil bulbs and 23 tulip bulbs.
How many bulbs are there altogether in the packet? 47

24
+23
---
47

**2** A bike has two wheels.
How many wheels are there on nine bikes? 18

**3** On Monday Rachel buys 14 stickers. On Tuesday she buys double that number.
How many stickers does she buy on Tuesday? 28

14
+14
---
28

**4** James has a tube of 30 Zunts. He eats half of them.
How many Zunts has he left? 15

**5** There are 13 biscuits on a plate. Liam eats 4 of them and Sally eats 3 of them.
How many biscuits are left? 6

**6** A box has 56 pencils. Emma puts in another 8 pencils.
How many pencils are in the box now? 64

**7**  I am a number. If I add 7 to my number and double the answer I get 20. What am I?

3

© Photocopying this material is not permitted.

# Time problems 1

**1.** A basketball game started at 2:15 p.m. It lasted for 35 minutes.
What time did it end? 2:50

start: 2:15
end:

50
25

**2.** A bus passes the school every 5 minutes. The first bus passes at 8 o'clock.

How many more buses will pass in the next 30 minutes? 6

**3.** Playtime begins at 10:25. It ends at 10:50.

25 past 10

How long does playtime last? 25

**4.** In a test Ruth answers one question every 5 minutes.

How long does it take her to answer 8 questions? 40

**5.** After 1 a.m. a plane goes from Dublin to Frankfurt every 5 hours.

How many planes go from Dublin to Frankfurt in one day? 2

**6.** A train journey takes 2 hours 15 minutes. It ends at 1 p.m.
What time did the train leave the station? 10:45

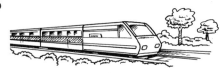

**7.**  I am between 8:20 and quarter to 9. My minutes are an odd multiple of 10. What am I?

8:30

# Number problems 3

**1** The result of a rugby match was 9 points to 4.

result 9 – 4

What was the points difference between the two scores? 5

**2** A baker has 10 tarts for sale. He sells two of them.

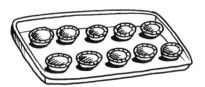

How many tarts has he left? 8

**3** Three children have come to Lisa's party. Soon 7 more children arrive.

How many children have come to Lisa's party? 10

**4** On one side of a road there are 4 houses. On the other side of the road there are 5 houses.

How many houses are there altogether on the road? 9

**5** Tommy sells 12 tickets for the school concert. Amy sells 8 tickets.

How many tickets have they sold altogether? 20

**6** Harry scores 16 points. He needs 20 points to win the game.

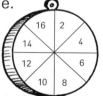

How many more points does he need to win the game? 4

**7**

*I have two digits. My units digit is 2. I am less than 20.*

What am I? 12

# Length problems 1

**1)** In a 400 metres race a runner has 100 metres left to run. How many metres has she run? 300 meters

32cm.
+27cm
59

**2)** Áine cuts a piece of ribbon into two lengths, 32 cm and 27 cm. How long was the ribbon before she cut it? 59 cm

**3)** A 28 cm length of wood is cut into two equal lengths.

What is the length of each piece? 14 cm

**4)** A tape measure is marked in metres on one side. On the other side it is marked in centimetres.

How many centimetres are on the other side to 2.5 metres? 250 cm

**5)** A bike race is 2 times around a 125 metres track. How long is the race? 256 metres

125.

**6)** A 40 cm lamp is put on a 1 metre high table. What is the height of the top of the lamp from the ground? 140 cm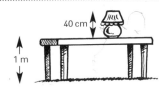

**7)**  I am a length between 3 and 6 metres. My length in cm has 3 even digits which are all the same. What am I? 444

# Review problems 1

**Marathon result**
1. J O'Leary 367 2 hr 17 min
2. S Collins 746 2 hr 19 min
3. F Reilly 607 2 hr 39 min
4. H Murphy 271 2 hr 58 min
5. R Smith 712 3 hr 08 min

**Ladies Long Jump result**
1. W O'Neill 692 11 m 33 cm
2. B Kubrick 489 11 m 17 cm
3. N Roster 361 10 m 40 cm
4. R Flynn 279 10 m 11 cm
5. T Malone 481 9 m 48 cm

**Entrance**
Adult €5
Children €2
School groups €30 per class

1. What is the entrance cost for a family of 2 adults and 3 children?
2. St. Kevin's Primary School brings 3 classes to the athletics meeting. How much does it cost the school?
3. Which runner in the marathon had 6 as the units digit of his number?
4. What is the number of the jumper in the long jump that has an odd hundreds digit?
5. In the marathon 300 runners started the race, but only 250 finished. How many did not finish the race?
6. A child from St. Kevin's School said, 'It would take me twice as long as R Smith to run the marathon.' How long is that?
7. By how many minutes did J O'Leary win the marathon?
8. The sixth finisher in the marathon finished 60 minutes after the winner. What was his finishing time?
9. By how many centimetres did W O'Neill win the long jump?
10. How many centimetres did R Flynn jump?
11. Seán estimated the number of people watching to be 200. The actual number was 700 more than this. How many were watching the athletics?
12. At the start of the athletics there were 70 cars in the car park. In the next hour another 30 cars arrived. How many cars were in the car park at that time?
13. There were 10 coaches in the coach park. Each coach had 50 people. How many people came in coaches?

# Number problems 4

**1** The houses on one side of a street have odd numbers in order. Karl lives in Number 1.

Alice lives four houses from Karl.
What is Alice's number? 9

**2** Louise puts out her toy sheep together in twos. She does this seven times.

How many sheep does she put out altogether? 14

**3** On a sheet of paper is a grid of 1 cm squares. The grid has 3 rows and 7 columns.
How many 1 cm squares are on the paper? 21

**4** Niamh planned her birthday party. She invited 15 girls and 4 boys, but 6 of them could not come.

How many children came to her party? 13

**5** At an airport 18 people are waiting to get on a plane. There are only 6 passenger seats left.

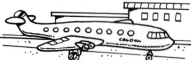

How many will not be able to get on the plane? 12

**6** Rob has 12 coins in his piggy bank. He is given 3 more coins.

How many coins has he now? 15

**7**  I am a two-digit number. My tens digit is half of my units digit. Both digits are even and less than 8.   What am I?

# Money problems 2

**1.** A bus ticket costs 65c. How much would two tickets cost?

**2.** Nadia has two 10c coins and one 50c coin. How much more does she need to buy an 80c ice cream?

**3.** Sarah's mum buys both the television and the DVD player.

How much does she pay?

**4.** Harry uses a €10 note to buy a €7 Gameboy.

How much change does he get?

**5.** Darragh's dad has saved €600 to buy the car. He is saving €100 each week. For how many more weeks does he need to save?

**6.** Síle saves 20c of her pocket money every week. How many euro will she have saved after 10 weeks?

**7.**  I am an amount of money. The total of one each of every kind of coin makes me. What am I?

# Number problems 5

1. Gary scores 6 points in a football match. Emma scores 10 more points than Gary. How many points does Emma score? 16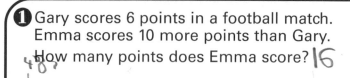

2. Children are taken on holiday in 100 taxis. Each taxi has 4 children. How many children go on holiday? 400

3. On Monday 487 planes land at an airport. On Tuesday 100 more land than on Monday. How many planes land on Tuesday? 587

4. Ailbhe sells 60 cakes at the school fair. This is 10 less than she estimated. How many did Ailbhe estimate she would sell? 70

5. In each box there are 20 pencils. How many pencils are there in 10 boxes? 200

6. Oisín sold 210 raffle tickets. Paddy sold 100 less than Oisín. How many raffle tickets did Paddy sell? 110

7. I am a two-digit even number. I am a multiple of 5. My tens digit is 8 more than my units digit. What am I? 80

# Number problems 6

odd
seven

**1** John breaks one of his four toy cars.

What fraction of his cars are broken? 3/4

**2** There are 40 dogs at a dog show. One-quarter of the dogs are poodles.

How many of the dogs are poodles? 10

**3** Bohemenians score 6 goals in a football match. Shamrock Rovers score half that number.

How many goals do Shamrock Rovers score? 3

**4** Helen has 15 stickers. Emma has double that.

How many stickers has Emma? 30

**5** A storm breaks one-tenth of the 200 windows in a block of flats.

How many windows are broken in the flats? 20

**6** Jake makes 8 sandwiches. His mother says that they need double that number.

How many sandwiches are needed? 16

**7**  I am a fraction. My top number is 1 less than my bottom number. My top number is the smallest even number. What am I?  1/2

# Time problems 2

**1)** Children go to a school for 37 weeks in each year.

How many weeks holiday do the children have in a year? 12 weeks

**2)** Darren can stand on one leg for 1 min 40 sec.

For how many more seconds does Darren need to stand on one leg to do it for 2 minutes? 20 sec

**3)** In a whole day Lucia sleeps for 11 hours.

For how many hours is Lucia awake in the day? 13

**4)** Jenny goes on her roller skates for a 1 hour ride.

How long has she still to go after 51 minutes? 9 min

**5)** When going on holiday Eimear spends 9 hours on a plane and 4 hours on a ship.

How many hours does she travel altogether? 13

**6)** Ivan watches two TV programmes. The first lasts for 25 minutes, the second for 26 minutes.

For how long does he watch TV? 51 min

**7)** I am a two-digit number of minutes. The sum of the digits is 8. My units digit is 3 times my tens digit.

What am I? 38

© Photocopying this material is not permitted.

# Number problems 7

**1)** In a game of darts Claire needs 91 to win. She scores 89.

What number does she need to score to win? 2

**2)** In a school playground there are 402 children. At 9 o'clock 396 of them go into school.

How many children are left in the playground? 6

**3)** Peter shares 48 flowers equally into two vases.

How many flowers are in each vase? 24

**4)** There are 5 toes on a foot.

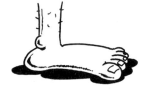 

How many toes are there on 7 feet? 35

**5)** Lucy has only 5c coins in her money box. Altogether she has 50c.
How many 5c coins has she in her money box? 10

**6)** Ten biscuits fit on each plate.
How many plates are needed for 80 biscuits? 8

**7)**  I am a two-digit number. I am double an odd number. My units digit is half of my tens digit. What am I?

# Review problems 2

1. A baby Diplodocus is 1 metre long.
   How many metres does it grow to become full size?
2. How many Dimetrodons make the same length as one Triceratops?
3. Write the names of the dinosaurs in order of length, longest first.
4. Write the names of the dinosaurs in order of weight, lightest first.
5. How many metres longer is a Tyrannosaurus rex than a Triceratops?
6. An egg laid by a Tyrannosaurus rex was like a very big sausage. It was 40 cm long and 15 cm wide. How many centimeters longer than wide was an egg?
7. A class of 30 children visit the museum. It costs each of them 50c to go in.
   What is the total cost for the 30 children?
8. The children walk in pairs to the museum.
   How many pairs do 30 children make?
9. The children take a lift to the café. The lift holds 10 children. How many times will the lift be needed to take all 30 children?
10. The class leave the school at half-past 10. They spend 4 hours out of school. At what time do they arrive back at school?
11. For how many hours is the museum open?

# Number problems 8

**1** Scoil Caitríona has 289 children. St. Mary's School has 298 children.

Which school has more children?
How many more?

**2** There are 13 people on a bus. At the next stop 8 more get on.

How many people are on the bus now?

**3** Along a road there are 14 lamps. Only 9 of them are working.

How many lamps are not working?

**4** On Thursday Peter laid 612 bricks. On Friday he laid 621 bricks.

On which day did he lay fewer bricks?
How many fewer?

**5** There are 9 flats in one block and 8 in the other block.

How many flats in the two blocks altogether?

**6** At a party there were 18 bottles of juice. The children drank 12 bottles.

How many bottles were not drunk?

**7**  I am between 100 and 200. My tens digit is 7. I am an odd multiple of 10  What am I?

# Money problems 3

**1** Jane buys a plant for her mum. The plant costs €3.80.
How much change does she get from €5?

**2** Tara buys a T-shirt for €2.90 and a cap for €1.50.
How much does she pay altogether?

**3** A parcel arrives at David's house. It has two stamps on it, a €2.50 and a 35c.
How much did the parcel cost to post?

**4** Adam and his dad go to the cinema.
How much does it cost?
How much change does Adam's dad get from a €10 note?

**5** Joanna wants to buy the box of chocolates for her mum. She has €2.60.
How much more does she need?

**6** Josh buys both games. He pays with a €10 note.
How much change does he get?

**7**
I am a money note.
I am between €10 and €50.
What am I?

# Number problems 9

**1** In a bag there are 12 oranges. A box of oranges has double that number.

How many oranges are in a box? 24

**2** There are 18 girls in a class. There are half as many boys as girls in the class.

How many boys are in the class? 9

**3** There are twice as many people on the upper deck of a bus as on the lower deck.
On the lower deck there are 19 people.
How many people are on the upper deck? 38

**4** A gardener plants trees at a school. She plants 18 trees at the front and 17 trees at the back of the school.
How many trees does she plant altogether? 35

**5** A squirrel has 34 nuts. He eats half of them.

How many nuts does he have left? 17

**6** When playing a game of darts Evan scores 13, 18 and 4.

What is his total score? 35

**7**  If you double me and then halve the answer you get 28. What am I? 56

# Time problems 3

```
 50    20
-35   +15
      35
```

**1** A candle lasts for 1 hour. James lights the candle at 9 o'clock.
How long will the candle stay lit after 9:45?  15 minutes

**2** A pie takes 35 minutes to cook. Meghan puts the pie in the oven at 10:50.
At what time will it be ready?

11:25

**3** A bus starts a journey at 9:45. The journey ends at 10:20.

35 minutes
For how many minutes does the journey last?

**4** In a triathlon Michelle swims for 25 minutes, runs for 15 minutes and cycles for 20 minutes.
How long does the whole race take?  an hour

**5** A train takes 25 minutes from Connolly station to Leixlip and 26 minutes from Leixlip to Enfield.
How long does it take from Connolly station to Enfield? 51 minutes

**6** Colm runs a mile race in 5 minutes 15 seconds. That is 20 seconds slower than Annie.
How long did it take Annie to run the mile race?
5 minutes 35 seconds

**7**

My hours are double 4.
My minutes are half of 40.

What am I?
8:20

# Weight problems 1

**1** Dave is baking. He uses 200 g out of a 1 kg packet of sugar.

How many grams of sugar are left? *800 g*

**2** A packet of crisps weighs 25 g.

What is the weight of two packets of crisps? *50 g*

**3** A packet of 5 tea bags weighs 25 g.

How much does one tea bag weigh? *5 g*

**4** Jamie buys the two pieces of cheese.

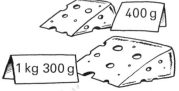

What is the total weight of the two pieces of cheese? *1 kg 700 g*

**5** At birth a puppy weighs 600 g. After 1 year it has increased its weight by 500 g.

How much does the puppy weigh after 1 year? *1 kg 100 g*

**6** A jar of jam weighs 400 g. How many kilograms do 5 jars weigh? *2 kg*

**7** My two digits are the same. Each digit is one-half of 10.

What am I? *55*

# Measures problems 1

**1)** In a pack there are 10 cans. Each can has 200 mL of juice.
How many litres of juice are there altogether in the pack?  2 litre

**2)** When training for a race Sinéad runs 500 m and jogs for 300 metres.
How many metres does she train for? 800 m

**3)** Ciarán does 10 step-ups every minute.
How long does it take Ciarán to do 100 step-ups? 10 mins

**4)** Alice weighs out 3 kg of flour. This is 200 g more than she needs.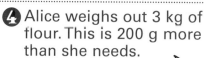
How much flour does she need? 2 kg 800 g

**5)** Aoife with her clothes on weighs 26 kg. Her clothes weigh 2 kg. A year later, without clothes, she weighs 29 kg.
By how many kilograms has her weight increased in the year? 4 kg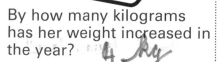

**6)** A balloon flies 100 metres each hour.
How far will the balloon fly in 8 hours? 800 m

**7)**  1 more than me is one-half of 500. What am I? 250

# Review problems 3

1. The swimming pool has 6 lanes.
   In which lane is the swimmer who is first?
   In which lane is the swimmer who is last?

2. The length of the pool is 50 metres.
   The race is 2 lengths of the pool.
   How long is the race?

3. The winner swims the first length in 31 sec and the second length in 29 sec.
   How long did it take him to swim the whole race?

4. Another race is 400 metres long.
   How many lengths of the pool is this?

5. Cillian and his mum and dad are watching.
   How much did it cost them to get in?

6. Cillian buys two lemon drinks.
   How much do they cost him?

7. How much more does an apple drink cost than orange?

8. A bottle of lemon has 300 mL.
   How many litres are in 10 bottles?

9. To get to the swimming pool Cillian walked 200 metres.
   He then went on a bus for 575 metres.
   How far did he go to get to the pool?

10. To get his Whale badge Cillian has to swim 4 lengths of the pool on his front and 4 lengths on his back.
    What is the total length he has to swim?

# Number problems 10

**1** A pack has 3 cans. Marta puts 4 packs in a pile.

How many cans are in the 4 packs? 12

**2** Two schools have a cross-country race. Each school has 5 runners.

How many children are in the race? 10

**3** In each box there are 4 cakes.
How many cakes are there altogether? 24

**4** There are 5 balls in a tube. Amy counts the number of balls in seven tubes.

How many balls will she count altogether? 35

**5** I start at a number and count on 2 threes and then 2 fours. I end at 15.

What number did I start at? 1

**6** In a red box there are 10 crayons. In a blue box there are twice as many as in the red box.
How many crayons are in the blue box? 20

**7**  I am a two-digit multiple of 3 and 4. My tens digit is 4. What am I? 48

# Money problems 4

**1** In a sale the price of the toaster is €5 less than its normal €18.
How much is the toaster in the sale? €13

**2** The table costs €400. The four chairs cost €600.

What is the total cost of the table and chairs? €1000

**3** Áine buys a 9c toffee and an 8c lolly.

How much does she pay altogether? 17c

**4** Greg has 12c. He buys a 4c sweet.
How much money has he left? 8c

**5** Marie pays €1.30 for an ice cream and 60c for an ice pop.

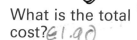

What is the total cost? €1.90

**6** Simon has saved €6.50. He needs another €3.50 to buy a CD.

How much is the CD? €10

**7**  I am two numbers. The total of my numbers is 1000. The difference between my two numbers is 100. What am I? 10

# Number problems 11

**1** Laura has 20 flowers to put into four vases. She shares them equally between the vases.
How many flowers are in each vase?

**2** A zoo has 248 animals. Another 100 animals are sent to the zoo.
How many animals are in the zoo now?

**3** In a nest there are 350 ants. At the end of the day 151 more ants return to the nest.
How many ants are in the nest at the end of the day?

**4** A class of 28 children are grouped into teams of 4.
How many teams are there?

**5** A supermarket sells 246 cans on a Monday. On Tuesday it sells 327.

Altogether how many cans does it sell on the two days?

**6** At the end of a party 30 balloons are shared equally between 10 children.

How many balloons does each child get?

**7**  *I am a three-digit number. My tens digit is 4. My units digit is half my tens digit. My hundreds digit is double my tens digit.* What am I?

# Number problems 12

**1** In a dish there are 8 strawberries. Debbie eats half of them. Adam eats two-quarters of them.

Who eats more?
Explain your answer.

**2** In a game Liam scores 40 points in 8 equal scores.

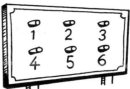

How many points does he score each time?

**3** A group of children is split into nine pairs.
How many children are in the group?

**4** Amy buys 5 stickers each week.
How many stickers has she at the end of 7 weeks?

**5** Joanne divides a bag of 14 apples equally between herself and her brother.
How many apples does her brother get?

14 apples

**6** Each packet has 3 cakes. Ciara buys 8 packets.
How many cakes does Ciara buy?

**7**  I am a three-digit number. The three digits are all different and in order, largest first. Each digit is a multiple of 3. What am I?

# Number problems 13

**1** Bill has 7 toy racing cars. Clara has double what Bill has. Clara gives Bill 3 of her cars.
How many cars has Clara left?

**2** Fionn buys a packet of 24 chews. He eats 4 of them and shares the rest equally between his 5 sisters.
How many chews does each get?

**3** There are 17 cars in a car park. Nine of the cars leave and 6 more come in.
How many cars are in the car park now?

**4** Sarah's mum has 2 packets of 8 ice lollies in the freezer.
Sarah eats 2 of the ice lollies.
How many are left?

**5** Aisling has 15 bird cards. She buys 5 packets of the bird cards. She finds she has 7 repeats so she gives them away.
How many has she left?

**6** Eoin buys and sells stamps. He already has 30 stamps. He buys 10 packets of 5 stamps. Then he puts all his stamps into packets of 5.
How many packets does he make?

**7** When I am subtracted from 80 the answer is double 35. What am I?

# Review problems 4

**1** A jumbo jet holds 400 passengers.
How many passengers can fit on 2 jumbo jets?
How many passengers are on a jumbo jet when it is half full?

**2** Write 125 cm as metres and centimetres.

**3** Tom's piece of string is 63 cm long. Nicola's piece is 37 cm long. What is the combined length of their strings?

**4** In 1 minute a fuel tanker could fill up the petrol tanks of 40 cars. A petrol tank of a car holds 50 litres.
How many litres can the fuel tanker put in the jumbo jet in one minute?

**5** For a long flight the jumbo jet is loaded with 800 meals. The jumbo jet has 400 passengers.
How many meals can each passenger have?

**6** A Concorde plane takes 3 hours to fly from Dublin to New York. A jumbo jet takes twice as long.
How long does it take for a jumbo jet to fly from Dublin to New York?

**7**  I am between 80 and 90. When you count on in fives starting at 0 you will say me. What am I?

# Number problems 14

**1** A red book has 273 pages. A blue book has 142 pages.

Which book has more pages?
How many more?

**2** In four games Jade scores 489, 483, 469 and 498 points.

Which was the most points Jade scored?
Which was the least points Jade scored?

**3** Maeve takes 35 strides to walk the length of the playground. Her brother takes twice as many strides.

How many strides did Maeve's brother take?

**4** Danny has a packet of 90 chocolate buttons. He eats half of them.

How many chocolate buttons does Danny have left?

**5** Paul is looking for his friend's home. He knows that it is an odd number between 159 and 163.

What number is it?

**6** With ten darts Sarah scores 205 points. Matthew scores 250 points with ten darts.

Who scored fewer points?
How many fewer?

**7**  I am a two-digit number. I am a multiple of 5 and 3. The difference between my digits is 1. What am I?

# Money problems 5

**1** Liam buys a violin for €120 and a trumpet for €80.

How much does he pay altogether for the two instruments?

**2** Seán sees the fishing rod for sale. He has €70.

How much more does he need?

**3** Claire gets €1.50 pocket money each week. On her birthday her dad gives her twice as much.

How much does her dad give her on her birthday?

**4** Conor saves 50c each week to buy the game Blitz.

How many weeks will it take to save enough money to buy the game?

**5** Jenny and her mum and dad go to the cinema.
What is the total cost?

Prices
Adults €3.50
Children €2.00

**6** Paula has €3. She spends half of it. Her mother then gives her 50c.

How much money does Paula have now?

**7**  I am more than €1.50 and less than €4.50. My amount in cent is a multiple of 3 and 50.

What am I?

# Number problems 15

**❶** There are 3 people on a bus. At the next three stops 3, 5 and 4 more people get on the bus.

How many people are on the bus now?

**❷** At the start of a film there are 39 children in the cinema. Soon 41 more have joined them.

How many children are in the cinema now?

**❸** Hugh gets 67 full glasses of juice ready for a party. Only 39 glasses are drunk.
How many full glasses are left?

**❹** Damian has 286 stamps in his album. He buys 33 more stamps.
How many stamps does he now have?

**❺** In the first game Aifric scores 127 points. In the second game she scores 455 points.

How many points does she score altogether?

**❻** There are 56 trees in a wood. In a conservation project children plant another 19 trees.

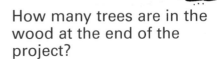

How many trees are in the wood at the end of the project?

**❼**  My 3 digits are odd and increase in size. All three digits are different. The sum of the digits is 9. What am I?

# Capacity problems 1

**1.** Lauren makes 17 litres of juice for a party. Her friends drink 12 litres.
How many litres of juice are left?

**2.** Cian mixes 800 mL of plant food in a bucket. He then mixes another 200 mL.
How many millilitres has he made altogether?

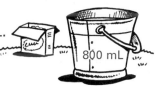

**3.** Each bottle has 1 L 500 mL of lemonade.

How many litres of lemonade are there in four bottles?

**4.** Gary is painting the house. He uses 7 litres of paint. He then uses another 8 litres.

How many litres did he use altogether?

**5.** A petrol can when full holds 10 litres. There are 3 L 300 mL in the can.

How much more petrol is needed to fill it?

**6.** Aaron has a cold. He has had 15 mL of medicine. He is given another 5 mL.

How many millilitres has he had altogether?

**7.**  Double me is 8 less than 40. What am I?

# Measures problems 2

**1** Cathal cuts a 1 metre piece of ribbon into five equal lengths.

How many centimetres long is each piece?

**2** Helen makes some Rice Crispie buns. She weighs out 85 g and then another 15 g.

How many grams of Rice Crispies does she weigh?

**3** A bottle holds 1 L 500 mL of water. A larger bottle holds twice as much water.

How many litres of water does the larger bottle hold?

**4** Every morning it takes Barry 15 minutes to walk to school.

How long does he spend walking to school in a week?

**5** Justin weighs out 3 kilograms of sugar. He divides the sugar equally into two basins.

How much sugar is in each basin?

**6** A train stops at the first station after 35 minutes. After 65 minutes it stops at the second station.

How long after the start is it before it stops for the second time?

**7**  I belong to the 2, 3 and 4 times-tables. The sum of my two digits is 9. What am I?

# Measures problems 3

**1.** A pack has 10 jars of beetroot. One jar weighs 300 grams.
What is the total weight of the pack?

**2.** The length of a bicycle race is three times along a street of a town. The race is 930 m long.
How long is it once along the street?

**3.** A test has 10 questions. It lasts 3 min 20 sec. Children have the same time to answer each question.

How long have the children to answer each question?

**4.** A bottle of vinegar when full holds 300 mL.

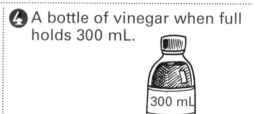

How many millilitres do 3 bottles hold?

**5.** A 10 metre length of wood is marked out into 10 equal lengths.

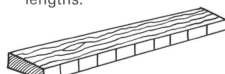

How many metres from one end is the third mark?

**6.** One bag of sugar weighs 1 kg. Jim opens three bags of sugar and divides it equally into ten bowls.

How many grams of sugar are in each bowl?

**7.**  Ten times me add 6 is 46. What am I?

# Review problems 5

1. The Punch and Judy show has started. Six more children come to watch.
   How many children are watching now?

2. Conor hires a motor boat for 1 hour.
   How much does it cost him?

3. Each pedal boat holds two people.
   How many people would 8 pedal boats hold?

4. John and Mary are building a sandcastle. John collects 4 buckets of water. Mary collects three times as many as John.
   How many buckets of water does Mary collect?

5. Each bucket of sand weighs 500 grams. It takes 10 full buckets to build a small castle.
   How many kilograms of sand are needed for a small castle?

6. Aly spends exactly €4 on cones and 99 cones.
   How many cones and 99 cones does she buy with the €4?

7. Ada buys 2 cones and 3 orange ice lollies.
   What is the total cost?

8. Tom has €5. How many 99 cones can he buy?
   How much change would he get?

9. There are 6 donkeys. In 30 minutes each donkey carries 5 children.
   How many children have a ride on 6 donkeys in one hour?

10. A donkey ride is 10 metres up and 10 metres back. How many times will a donkey have to go up and back to do 100 metres?

11. What is the cost of a deck chair for a whole day?

# Number problems 16

**1.** I am thinking of a number.
My number is the seventeenth multiple of 2.
What is my number?

**2.** I am thinking of a number.
My number is the sum of the eighth and the eleventh multiple of 10.
What is my number?

**3.** I am thinking of a number.
My number is one-half of the tenth multiple of 50.
What is my number?

**4.** I am thinking of a number.
My number is 17 more than the fifth multiple of 100.
What is my number?

**5.** I am thinking of a number.
My number is double the ninth multiple of 5.
What is my number?

**6.** I am thinking of a number.
My number is the first multiple of both 5 and 100.
What is my number?

**7.**  I am two numbers. The sum of my numbers is 15. The difference between my numbers is 3. What am I?

# Money problems 6

**1** Alex's mum and dad look at some TVs.

What is the cost of the cheapest TV?

What is the cost of the dearest TV?

**2** Kylie buys a soft rabbit for €13. She pays with a €20 note.

How much change does Kylie get?

**3** Simon keeps pet snakes. He buys 3 snakes at €20 each.

How much does Simon pay altogether?

**4** Four children go to the cinema. The total cost is €16.

What is the cost for one child?

**5** Fiona and her dad go swimming. It costs €4 for an adult and €2.50 for a child.

What is the total cost for Fiona and her dad?

**6** Christina has four €5 notes. She buys a toy monster for €7.

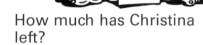

How much has Christina left?

**7**  If you add 7 to me and then take away 11 you will get 6.

What am I?

# Number problems 17

**1** Each box has 15 golf balls.

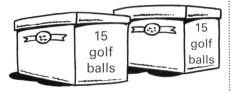

How many golf balls are in two boxes?

**2** Eighty children go on a school trip. One-half of the children are boys.

How many girls go on the trip?

**3** I think of a number.
Double my number plus 8 is 82.
What is my number?

**4** The Odeon cinema has 250 seats.
The Classic has double that number.
How many seats are in the Classic?

**5** In a bottle bank there are 700 bottles. Half of the bottles are green.

How many bottles are not green?

**6** Alice sells 250 raffle tickets. Holly sells 149.

How many tickets do Alice and Holly sell altogether?

**7**  Both my hundreds and units digits are one-half of my tens digit. The sum of my three digits is 16. What am I?

# Number problems 18

**1** Street School hope that 1000 people will come to the school fair. At the opening only 400 have come.
How many more have to come to make 1000?  **600**

**2** Mary eats $\frac{1}{2}$ of a cake. Niall eats $\frac{1}{4}$ of the cake.
Who eats more of the cake?
Write about how you found out.  **Mary**

**3** There are 85 hens on a farm. The farmer buys another 15 hens.

How many hens does the farmer have now? **100**

**4** There are 200 people at the afternoon circus show. In the evening there are 800 people.

How many people are at the two shows altogether? **1000**

**5** Marc has a box of jelly babies. He eats $\frac{1}{10}$ of them. Adam eats $\frac{1}{2}$ of them and Jessica eats $\frac{1}{4}$ of them.
Who eats the most sweets? **Adam**

**6** A hundred children have school milks. Thirty-five bring their own drinks.
How many more children have milks than bring their own drinks? **65**

**7**  My tens digit is half the sum of my other two digits. My units digit is 8 more than my hundreds digit.

What am I?

# Time problems 4

**1**

What day comes 19 days after a Monday?

**2** The months of July and August have 31 days.

How many days are there from 1st July to 31st August?

**3** Each team in a bicycle relay race has 6 riders. Each rider rides for 5 hours. The race starts at 9 a.m. on a Saturday.

When does the race end?

**4**

What is the date 21 days before 10th October?

**5** A man starts work on 1st July. He works for 5 days and rests for 5 days all the month.

For how many days does he rest between 1st July and 31st July?

**6** In 2002 Sarah's birthday was on Thursday, 14th February.
On which day was her birthday in 2003?
Which day was it in 2001?

**7** I am a day of the week. The number of letters in my name is not a multiple of 2, nor a multiple of 3. What am I?

# Number problems 19

**1)** There are 253 children in a school hall.
Six more children arrive late.
How many children are in the hall now? 259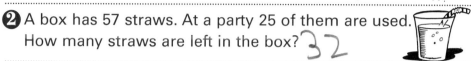

**2)** A box has 57 straws. At a party 25 of them are used.
How many straws are left in the box? 32

**3)** In four games of skittles Amy scores 8 points in each game.

How many points does she score altogether? 32

**4)** A trawler catches 138 crabs. The fisherman puts 50 of the crabs back into the sea.

How many crabs are left? 88

**5)** At a zoo there are 24 monkeys. The monkeys are divided equally between four enclosures.

How many monkeys are there in each enclosure? 6

**6)** Australia score 2 goals and 1 point. This is 1 more goal than Ireland scores.

What was Ireland's score? 1 Goal. 1 Point

**7)**  I am a multiple of 4 and 5.
I am between 21 and 59.
What am I?
40

# Review problems 6

**1)** In a 400 metres race Anna finishes 7 metres behind the winner.

How far has Anna run when the winner passes the winning post?

**2)** Ketchup in a bottle weighs 500 grams.

What is the total weight of ketchup in four bottles?

**3)** Jenny sends two parcels by post. One costs €2.70, the other costs €1.90.

What is the total cost of the two parcels?

**4)** A litre of juice is poured equally into two bottles.

How many millilitres of juice are in each bottle?

**5)** Joe catches a train at 12 o'clock. The journey lasts for 1 hr 30 min. He then takes a bus and gets home at 2 p.m.

How long does the bus journey take?

**6)** A packet has 20 biscuits. Four packets are put into a box. Sam eats six of the biscuits.
How many biscuits are left in the box?

**7)**  Three more than me is double 20. What am I?